BLUNDERS SINGLES MUST AVOID

MAJOR DAUGHTER

Blunders Singles Must Avoid

ISBN: 978-1-68411-365-1

Published and Distributed by

GraceWorld Books

Printed in the South Africa

TABLE OF CONTENTS

INTRODUCTION

CONCLUSION

INTRODUCTION

The bedrock of every society is the family. Every family contributes the various individuals that make up the entire members of any particular society. For that society to be vibrant and whole, the various families in that society must also be vibrant and whole.

Now for a family to be able to contribute responsible citizens to the society, the husband and wife must be responsible. This can only be achieved if the man or woman allows the Spirit and the Word of God to guide them in choosing the right partner for marriage.

The reason divorce is prevalent in most modern societies is because couples fail to allow God's Word to guide them. They build their marriage on the principles of the world that are designed to fail at the slightest challenge. If the intending couples are mindful of these common blunders, they will marry the right partners and have enduring marriages.

CHAPTER 1

HAVING A SELFISH MOTIVE

There is such a thing as the good, acceptable and perfect will of God. Romans 12:2 says, *"And be not conformed to this world, but be transformed by the renewing of [your] mind, that ye may prove what [is] the good and acceptable and perfect will of God."* In other words, God's good will is different than an acceptable will, and God's perfect will is also very different from the previous wills.

If you want to make a choice for a life partner, ask God for His perfect will for you. It is a big blunder to already have someone in mind or to be in a relationship with someone and ask God to make that person His will for you. In that kind of scenario, you are trying to force God's hand to accept your choice instead of His choice for you.

Have you heard of some sisters who use pregnancy to force a brother to marry them? They get involved in fornication, get pregnant and leave their pastor with no choice than to ask them to finalize the marriage rites outside of church and to later come for a marriage blessing. This is likened to the good will of God because the pastor was forced to accept the union.

Those who have their specifications for a marriage partner outlined or have someone ready but ask the church or pastor to approve the partner for marriage without asking if that is God's will for them, fall into the acceptable will category. They could even have met their partner on the street, in a club, at the office or even in church but they refuse to seek godly counsel concerning their choice. This is very dangerous.

When you sincerely pray to God for a life partner or when you go to your pastor to guide you by the leading of the Holy Spirit, this is the perfect will of God. Those who do this hardly make any mistake in their choices. And they are the ones with enduring marriages.

CHAPTER 2

NOT ALLOWING YOUR VIRTUES TO PLAY THEIR ROLE

It is important to be conscious of your God-given virtues or talents. If you misuse them, you could end up missing out in life or not able to fulfill your God-given purpose in life. The Word of God says, *"But godliness with contentment is great gain,"* 1 Timothy 6:6. Be content with using your talent to please God. There are those who can sing very well and they actually started singing in church. However, they got misled to leave the church for the world and for so-called fame. While thinking they had arrived, the devil led them into marrying wolves in sheep's clothing, and that is where their problems and downfall started.

There are others who completely miss the opportunity to marry the right person because of their attitudes. So many have been left frustrated in life because of their pride, arrogance, anger, bitterness and so on. They prayed for years for a marriage partner but when the partner showed up, their dirty attitude made them miss out. They drove their partners away with their anger, pride or arrogance without knowing it.

"A man's gift will make room for him and bring him before the great,"
Proverbs 18:16

The gift of God is meant to bless you and not to cause you sorrow. Cultivate a good attitude towards others. Also learn to be hospitable because it is possible you might unknowingly be entertaining your future spouse or someone who will introduce you to him or her.

"Do not neglect to show hospitality to strangers, for thereby some have entertained angels unawares,"
Hebrews 13:2

There are so many who have met their spouses by showing an act of kindness or help to them. God is not restricted. He can guide your partner to you whichever way He pleases.

CHAPTER 3

THINKING SEX IS A GUARANTY

A lot of Christian singles make the blunder of engaging in premarital sex as a way of capturing or securing a partner for marriage. This is a lie sold by the devil. Sex is not a guaranty that a partner will marry you. In fact, in most cases, it has led to many ladies being disappointed. After the man has had his fill, he does not see anything worth marrying the lady for. He drops her and moves to the next available lady.

The Word of God says, to the one you are joined, you are one body with that person.

> *"Or do you not know that he who is joined to a prostitute becomes one body with her? For, as it is written, "The two will become one flesh,"*
> 1 Corinthians 6:16

Can you see that? The implication of sleeping with different partners before marriage is that you become one with them; you become fused in body, soul and spirit with whomever you have slept with. If the person is possessed by a demon, you become a partaker of the demon and its problems.

Furthermore, premarital sex is a sin against God. If a marriage is built on the foundation of sin, that marriage is bound to hit the rocks.

MAJOR DAUGTHER 6

"Let marriage be held in honor among all, and let the marriage bed be undefiled, for God will judge the sexually immoral and adulterous,"
Hebrews 13:4

Interestingly, most men value ladies who are virgins. Those are the ones they would rather marry than the ladies who have had several partners. So, strive to maintain your virginity till you are married.

CHAPTER 4

SPIRITUAL ENTANGLEMENT

To many singles out there, this mistake might be perceived as a hoax. The reason is that they are sense ruled, not able to understand spiritual verities. Well, whether you believe it or not, it is possible. And it is what is keeping so many singles unmarried and where they are married, the union is beset with myriads of problems. The scripture we read earlier readily comes to mind.

> *"Or do you not know that he who is joined to a prostitute becomes one body with her? For, as it is written, 'The two will become one flesh,'"*
> 1 Corinthians 6:16

In the same way an individual can get sexually transmitted diseases or infections from another partner, a Christian single can get spiritually entangled to demons and other spiritual wickedness if he or she had fellowship with a person possessed with demons; was dedicated to an idol; ate food dedicated to these demons or idols; harbored sin in his or her life, etc.

If an individual is dedicated to an idol knowingly or unknowingly, the man or woman automatically becomes the property of demons controlling the idol. It is these demons that keep the individual from getting married. They cast a spell on the person so he or she becomes unmarriageable. In a situation where these people succeed in getting married, they might remain childless or give birth to a child who causes a series of problems.

The remedy to these kinds of problems is for the person affected to cast out the demons from his or her life. To do this, the person must be apt to studying God's Word so he or she can know the rights, privileges, and authority he or she has in Christ Jesus. Another thing the individual can do is to cease any kind of fellowship with the people or places that led him or her into the satanic attacks.

CHAPTER 5

DEALING WITH MEDIUMS

"Do not turn to mediums or spiritists; do not seek them out to be defiled by them. I am the LORD your God,"
Leviticus 19:31

This is a very serious blunder that some Christian singles make. They foolishly consult mediums and diviners to show them their life partners. Of course if you go to the devil for a solution, he will give you something counterfeit—something that seemingly looks good and real but in the end will destroy you. Proverbs 14:12 lets us know that: *"There is a way that seems right to a man, but its end is the way to death."* The devil or his agent cannot point someone for you to marry and you would believe it is for real. The Word of God calls him a liar and the father of all lies. Whatever he gives you will definitely look like glitter but it is a time bomb waiting for the right opportunity to explode.

Again, the right thing to do when making a choice for a wife or a husband is to go to the Lord. He is the one who created you. Therefore, He knows the right lady or man for you. Refuse to be tempted or lured by the devil or his agents. The Word of God says, "Thus says the LORD; Cursed be the man that trusts in man, and makes flesh his arm, and whose heart departs from the LORD," Jeremiah 17: 5. For a Christian single to have any dealings with mediums, witch doctors, psychics, diviners, spiritists, occultists and astrologers means he or she has turned from the Lord to familiar spirits. His or her trust for the best is no longer on the Lord, but on the devil.

In 1 Samuel 28:3-25, we read how King Saul consulted a woman who was a medium in En Dor to conjure up the spirit of the Prophet Samuel. Sure, the medium woman brought up what seemed like the spirit of Prophet Samuel, but it was a familiar spirit. Interestingly, some Christians use this example as an excuse to deal with sorcerers, diviners and the likes. This is wrong and it can never point you to God's best for you.

CHAPTER 6

NOT KNOWING YOUR AUTHORITY IN CHRIST

As a Christian single, it is very important you know your rights and authority in Christ Jesus. If you do not know them or if you fail to exercise your authority, the devil will rob you of your blessings. The word of God says, *"Therefore, if anyone is in Christ, he is a new creation. The old has passed away; behold, the new has come,"* 2 Corinthians 5:17. Refuse to allow yourself to be ensnared with the yoke of "unbroken covenants." In other words, do not make a mountain out of a molehill. Now that you are in Christ, every other covenant consciously or unconsciously entered is broken. You have entered into a superior covenant with the Lord Jesus Christ. You are no longer bound by the so called "covenant of sex with first partner or any blood covenant."

However, if you do not know the efficacy of the new covenant you have entered with Christ and how it has liberated you from guilt, pains, traumas and bad memories of the ungodly relationships you had in the past, the devil will taunt you and make you feel you are still tied to those covenants. Therefore, voraciously go for the Word, the perfect law of liberty.

"My people are destroyed for lack of knowledge; because you have rejected knowledge, I reject you from being a priest to me. And since you have forgotten the law of your God, I also will forget your children,"

Hosea 4:6

CHAPTER 7

YOUR APPEARANCE DOES NOT COUNT

The way you dress as a female or male Christian single does matter. It is misleading to conclude that you can dress the way you like and still attract the best partner for marriage. There is the saying that "your attitude will determine your altitude in life." How true. Even as a man, if you do not dress well, no one will take you seriously. You will pass for an irresponsible man.

If you are a lady, do not dress like a harlot and expect to attract a responsible suitor for marriage. The Word of God says, ***"Likewise, I want the women to adorn themselves with respectable apparel, with modesty, and with self-control, not with braided hair or gold or pearls or expensive clothes, but with good deeds, as is proper for women who profess to worship God,"*** 1 Timothy 2:9–10.

Dressing well goes beyond wearing nice or expensive clothes. It is also very important you take your personal hygiene seriously. Bathe well and at least twice a day. If you know you have the tendency to sweat a lot and to smell with body odor, take extra care of yourself. Use good deodorant or perfume after bathing. Note that bad smell attracts demons and can drive away a potential suitor. Also ensure your clothes are ironed and your shoes polished. This way, you will always look good.

Another aspect you must not neglect is the way you carry yourself. Stop seeing yourself as a nobody. You are a child of God, and thus very important. Learn to talk right and behave decently whether you are being watched or alone. Remember, you are fearfully and wonderfully made, and you are God's best.

CHAPTER 8

BELIEVING IN DATING AND MATCHMAKING SITES

What on earth would a Christian single brother or sister be doing on dating and matchmaking sites to get a partner? That is unbelievable! I am averse to even Christian matchmaking sites. Marriage and who you marry are serious issues and it is important you know the person you want to spend the rest of your life with to a large extent. Anyone seriously considering a lifelong commitment would not expect to find that partner on some dating and matchmaking site.

"Now flee from youthful lusts and pursue righteousness, faith, love and peace, with those who call on the Lord from a pure heart,"
2 Timothy 2:22

The same goes for social media. You cannot seriously be considering marriage with someone you met on any of the social media platforms. So many have met with their early death going on a date with someone they met on social media. To consider courtship or marriage with someone you met chatting on some social media site is dangerous. Beware!

If you are really serious about who to marry, look inward. There are so many good and suitable candidates in your local church.

And if you are not comfortable approaching anyone, go to your pastor for advice and assistance. Your pastor has been anointed to be able to discern and assist you with the right brother or sister. Besides, your pastor is the one with spiritual authority over you, the one who watches over your soul. He is therefore the best person to recommend a wife or husband for you.

Also, you must be careful about matchmakers in and around you. They are in your community, office, family and even church. If the person is not the one with spiritual authority over you as in your pastor, be careful. The Word of God says, ***"Do not be deceived: "Bad company corrupts good morals,"*** 1 Corinthians 15:33. In other words, if you consult people who are spiritually and morally bankrupt for a marriage partner, they will only recommend their type to you. Sweet water cannot come out of a bitter fountain.

CHAPTER 9

HIS OR HER BACKGROUND DOES NOT COUNT

Do not make the blunder of not checking out the background of whoever you have decided to marry. The reason this is important is so that you understand the person, his or her orientation, beliefs, spiritual connections, etc. So many have made the blunder of thinking because they met the brother or sister in church that would suffice.

There are people from backgrounds where marriage is not held in high regard. They only stay when it is rosy and at the time of serious challenge, they are out. Some persons are from the background where not much regard is given to women. They do not see wife battering as anything wrong. Likewise, there are ladies from homes where they treat their husbands with disdain. They can publicly insult and embarrass their husbands because that is how women from their background treat their husbands.

Another reason it is important you check the background of the man or lady you intend to marry is to find out if the brother or sister still has any connections to idols or deities that might impair your marriage. Of course the brother or sister is now born again as far as you know. However, still check if he or she still has any connections or affiliations in any form. The reason this is important is that though these fellows come to church, some still secretly directly or indirectly worship these devils. The implication of this is that those evil spirits will come fighting the marriage. They could make child-bearing difficult. When couples do not know their right in Christ or fail to exercise their authority, demons will afflict them with sicknesses and several other challenges. So, do not be clouded with love and fantasy; checkout that fellow before you say, "I do."

HOW TO PRAY FOR A LIFE PARTNER

DAY 1

Dear heavenly Father, I thank You for Your Word and the examples it has set for us to follow. Lord, I am determined to walk in Your perfect will for me. And I pray for the guidance of the Holy Spirit in choosing a life partner. Thank You Father, in Jesus' Name I pray. Amen.

DAY 2

Thank You Most Holy Father for the brother/sister You have ordained from the beginning of time to be my spouse. I declare that I am led by the Holy Spirit to meet her/him. I will not make any blunder, but by Your leading, I will meet and be able to recognize him/her, in Jesus' Name. Amen

---

DAY 3

Precious Father, I thank You for my future spouse. With thanksgiving, I receive him/her. Lord, I pray that together we will fulfil Your plans and purposes for our lives. Our marriage will be a godly example that all will see and give glory to Your Holy Name, in Jesus' Name I pray. Amen.

DAY 4

Thank You heavenly Father for the beautiful life of marital bliss You have prepared for me. Your Word says, "He that finds a wife, finds a good thing and obtains favor from the Lord." Lord, I thank You because my spouse is a blessing and a favor from You to me. In Jesus' Name. Amen.

DAY 5

Father in the Name of Jesus Christ, I declare that I am full of patience. I discipline myself with Your Word and thus refuse to be hasty in making a decision on who to marry. Your Word is a lamp unto my feet and a light unto my path. Therefore, I submit myself under the ministry of Your Word and Spirit. Thus, I am able to do the right thing to Your praise and glory. Amen.

CONCLUSION

F inding a godly lady or man to marry is not a mystery at all. In fact, it is the easiest thing to achieve if one is truly sincere about it. Remember what the Word of God says in Proverbs 18:22 it says, ***"He who finds a wife finds a good thing and obtains favor from the LORD."*** Can you see that? It follows that if you allow the Spirit of God to guide you; you will find a good wife or husband and obtain favor from the Lord.

So, stop thinking that getting a good wife or husband is a mountain too high to climb. They are in your local church. Approach an elder or a deacon or your pastor for assistance. This is the right thing to do and the best way to get God's choice for you. Again, remember that God always wants the best for you.